AIRCRAFT

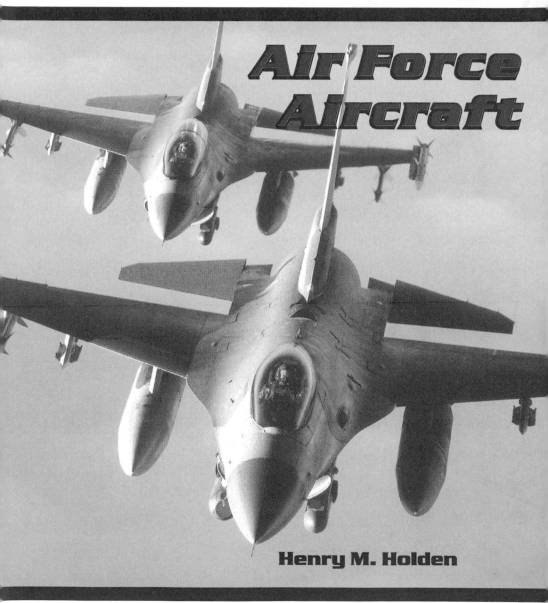

Air Force Aircraft

Henry M. Holden

Enslow Publishers, Inc.

40 Industrial Road	PO Box 38
Box 398	Aldershot
Berkeley Heights, NJ 07922	Hants GU12 6BP
USA	UK

http://www.enslow.com

To my grandaughter, Maura, with love.
Someday you will fly with the eagles.

Copyright © 2001 by Henry M. Holden

Library of Congress Cataloging-in-Publication Data

Holden, Henry M.
    Air Force aircraft / Henry M. Holden.
      p. cm. — (Aircraft)
    Includes bibliographical references (p.   ) and index.
    ISBN 0-7660-1714-1
    1. Airplanes, Military—United States—Juvenile literature. 2. United States.
Air Force—Juvenile literature. [1. Airplanes, Military. 2. United States. Air Force.]
I. Title. II. Series: Aircraft (Berkeley Heights, N.J.)
UG1243.H65 2001
358.4'183—dc21

                                                                00-010053

Printed in the United States of America

10 9 8 7 6 5 4 3 2 1

To Our Readers: All Internet Addresses in this book were active and appropriate
when we went to press. Any comments or suggestions can be sent by e-mail to
Comments@enslow.com or to the address on the back cover.

Photo Credits: United States Air Force

Cover Illustration: United States Air Force

Contents

CHAPTER 1

Air Force One

UNITED STATES O

Boeing 747-200B

The mission of Air Force One is to provide air transportation for the President of the United States. Any plane the President is on is called Air Force One. Only U.S. Air Force pilots are allowed to fly this airplane. The President uses Air Force One to visit people in the United States, to conduct business with international leaders, to visit foreign countries, and to travel on vacation.

Air Force One is a Boeing 747-200B with many special features. On each side of Air Force One are the words *United States of America*, along with the presidential seal. Even though it is the same size as a regular 747, about 232 feet long, it does not look like a regular airplane inside. It has an office for the President, a conference room that is as large as the one in the White House, a dining room, and sleeping quarters for the President and the First Lady. The President's bedroom has twin beds and a bathroom with a shower. Guests, senior staff, Secret Service personnel, and the news media have separate accommodations. Air Force One has leather seats, wood-grained furniture, and paneling similar to what is found in the White House.[1] Next to the President's office is a medical room, complete with an operating table and equipment to treat medical emergencies.

Air Force One has four jet engines and can fly 9,600 miles without refueling. That is the distance from Miami, Florida, to Sydney, Australia. It has almost as much communications equipment as the White House does. There are 85 telephones, 57 antennas, 19 television sets, 11 videocassette players, and several computers that can communicate with computers on the ground. There are more than 230 miles of electrical wiring, more than twice the amount in a normal 747. The communications equipment permits the President to get information from

Air Force One stands six stories high. It has four jet engines, and can fly 9,600 miles without refueling. It also has 85 telephones, 57 antennas, 19 television monitors, 11 videocassette players, and several computers.

satellites or to communicate with submarine commanders. "Anything that the President or the White House staff can do on the ground, we can do in the air," said former Air Force One Communications Chief Joe Jaworski.[2]

Air Force One cost $300 million, stands six stories high, and flies at approximately 550 miles per hour. It is the most powerful and visible symbol of the United States when the President is traveling. "I would get goose bumps whenever I saw it," said Henry Kissinger, former secretary of state.

"No matter what country we were in, the President would always come aboard and say how good it was to be back in a piece of America," said retired Chief Master Sergeant Charlie Palmer, a former chief steward on Air Force One.[3]

The food on Air Force One is tasty but not fancy. Two kitchens, or galleys, can provide up to one hundred meals at one sitting. Freezers on board hold enough food for a week. In an emergency, the President could live on the plane for seven days.

Air Force One can take the President anywhere in the world at a moment's notice. "There is nothing to compare to Air Force One," said former president Gerald Ford. "In any emergency, and under any conditions, the technical equipment that is in it is just like in the White House."

The President's plane never travels alone. Other support aircraft accompany Air Force One. They fly miles apart so that they do not endanger the President. They carry vehicles, personnel, and security equipment. At least one presidential helicopter, Marine One, travels with him and is ready to fly him to a hospital if he has a medical emergency. Often he travels with dozens of planes. When President Bill Clinton traveled to India in March 2000, seventy-six Air Force aircraft escorted him.

Safety of the President is the number one concern on Air Force One. Air Force One never travels with fighter plane escorts. Because fighter planes would have to fly too close to the President's plane, the Secret Service is afraid there could be a midair crash.[4] When Air Force One is at home, it sits in a high-security hangar at Andrews Air Force Base, Maryland. Even the pilots have to get special permission to board the airplane.[5]

Air Force One generally fuels up at Andrews Air Force Base. As a safety precaution, the fuel is tested and set aside in a locked tanker jet used only for Air Force One. This tanker flies with Air Force One and refuels the President's airplane in flight if necessary.

Air Force One also carries top secret military equipment. It has electronic equipment that can jam enemy radar and other communications systems. If someone were to shoot a missile at Air Force One, the crew could shoot off flares to drive the heat-seeking missiles away from the plane. It could also release thousands of small aluminum strips called chaff, which would help hide the airplane from radar. Chaff creates thousands of false radar images to confuse the operators.

When Air Force One is on final approach to landing at an airport, all airport activity stops. All planes scheduled to land circle instead, and no plane takes off until the President is safely on the ground.

There are actually two identical airplanes called "Air Force One." The only difference between them is their tail numbers. One is 28000 and the other is 29000.

The Air Force One call sign was first used in 1959 after there had been confusion between an Eastern Airlines flight and the President's plane. The President's airplane could have had a serious accident, so from then on any airplane the President was flying in became known as Air Force One.

There are actually two identical airplanes called Air Force One. The only difference between them is their tail numbers. One is 28000 and the other is 29000. When the President is aboard either aircraft, or any Air Force aircraft, the radio call sign is Air Force One. When the Vice President travels on one, it is called Air Force Two. When the First Lady travels alone on the airplane, the crew uses its tail number as its call sign.

A total of twelve presidents have flown on airplanes. President Franklin D. Roosevelt, in 1944, was the first president to use an airplane to travel. His airplane was a four-engine military transport called a C-54. Then came a Douglas DC-6, which flew President Harry S. Truman between 1947 and 1953. President Dwight D. Eisenhower traveled aboard a four-engine Lockheed Constellation from 1953 to 1961. President John F. Kennedy used a Boeing 707.

The current Air Force One was delivered in 1990, to then President George Bush. When he was asked what the plane was really like, he replied, "Well, let me tell you: it's grand. It's not fancy, . . . But man oh man, is it comfortable."[6]

The primary purpose of the Air Force is to defend America from the air. In addition to flying Air Force One, it flies fighters, bombers, transport airplanes, and special airplanes that are used as spy planes.

CHAPTER 2

Fighters

"I had mixed emotions . . . the evening of January 16, 1991," said Colonel Greg Feest, a stealth F-117A fighter pilot, ". . . In the back of my mind I wondered . . . would this stealth technology really work? After all, we were flying into the heart of the Iraqi air defense system."

Colonel Feest was on the first mission in Operation Desert Storm, a war between the United States and Iraq. The F-117A fighter jet had never been flown before in combat, and Feest wondered if the black jet would really be invisible to enemy radar.

Fighter planes are one- and two-seat jet airplanes that carry both bombs and missiles.

They attack ground targets, such as tanks. They also battle enemy fighter planes in the air. Some fighters carry their weaponry on their wings. Other fighters, especially stealth planes such as the F-117A Nighthawk and the F-22 Raptor, carry their missiles or bombs inside their fuselage. Missiles are used to shoot down enemy airplanes, and bombs are used to destroy enemy targets on the ground. The F-117A does not attack other planes, but it does carry bombs.

≡ The F-117A Nighthawk

The F-117A was the first stealth fighter plane in the Air Force. An aircraft with stealth means that the craft becomes very difficult to detect using radar or heat sensors (infrared). Stealth planes are almost completely invisible to radar. Radar works by sending out a beam of energy in the form of radio waves. When the beam hits an airplane, it bounces back to the radar site. The radar operator sees a spot or a "blip" on the radar screen and knows there is an airplane out there.

The F-117A does not look like a regular airplane with rounded surfaces. It is made with flat panels, placed at angles, to scatter the radar energy away from the airplane and out into space. Its shape is like a diamond with many flat sides. Because of the flat panels, the F-117A does not bounce the radar beam back to the radar site, so there is no blip on the screen.

There is just one pilot in the F-117A. He relies on the airplane's stealth technology to escape enemy detection.[2]

The F-117A stealth fighter has no curves. The flat sides deflect radar waves, making the plane "invisible."

The Air Force flies it only at night on bombing missions. Because it is such a large, visible target in the daytime, the only way to hide it is to paint it flat black and fly it at night.[3]

At twenty-two minutes after midnight, on January 17, 1991, the first wave of ten F-117A fighters code-named Thunder took off under radio silence to bomb Baghdad, Iraq.[4] *Radio silence* means the pilots do not talk to anyone on the radio. They did not want to warn the Iraqis they were coming. At 2:30 A.M. they topped off their tanks, from an aerial tanker, replacing the fuel they had used.

Approximately twenty minutes later, flying at close to 650 miles per hour, they dropped the first bombs of Operation Desert Storm.

The targets—military airfields and bridges—were just outside Baghdad and were easy to find on the airplane's radar. There was no antiaircraft fire coming up from Baghdad. "It appeared that no one knew I was in the sky," said Colonel Feest.

After locating the target, Feest aimed the crosshairs of his weapons system on the bridge and depressed a button on his control stick. Then the computers took over.

"My laser began to flash as I tracked the target," said Feest. "I waited for the display to tell me I was in range, and I pressed the Pickle button." The Pickle button is a nickname for the bomb release. "I felt the weapons bay doors snap open, and I felt the two-thousand-pound bomb drop from the aircraft. The doors slammed shut, and I watched on my infrared screen as the bomb went through the target."

With the bridge destroyed, Colonel Feest headed for the next target. The colonel's wingman was flying behind him in another F-117A. The wingman made sure no enemy fighters sneaked up from behind Colonel Feest. As the colonel looked back to check on his wingman, he could see what looked like fireworks lighting up the sky. A moment later he realized it was antiaircraft fire. The Iraqis had fired after the bombs had hit, but the F-117As were already clear of the target.

"Stealth technology really worked," said Colonel Feest.

The Iraqis tried to stop the attacks by launching hundreds of surface-to-air missiles (SAMs). SAMs are launched from the ground and seek the heat of a jet engine. If they can lock on to the jet's exhaust, they can hit the airplane. But the SAMs did no good. It took only 36 F-117As to destroy the military headquarters in Baghdad, as well as underground bunkers, bridges, and most of Saddam Hussein's important communications and radar sites in the first few nights.

F-16s have long pointed wings, a long tail, and a pointy nose. They have the ability to carry heavy artillery (as seen on its wings).

The stealth fighters flew 1,300 combat missions in Operation Desert Storm. Not one F-117A was shot down or even got a scratch. The F-117A was undetectable.

The F-16 Fighting Falcon

The F-16 Fighting Falcon is another Air Force fighter jet. It is a single-seat fighter. The pilot sits high up in a bubblelike canopy surrounding the cockpit so that he can see great distances around him. The Falcon is 49 feet long and can fly to 50,000 feet at speeds of up to 1,500 miles per hour, or Mach 2, which is twice the speed of sound.

One of the jobs of the F-16 is to protect the bombers that are bombing enemy targets. It does this with the air-to-air missiles it carries on its wings. It can also drop bombs on ground targets. Fighters such as the F-16 can fly upside down and make quick movements to escape enemy missiles.

The U.S. Air Force Thunderbirds

The Air Force Thunderbirds fly complicated and thrilling aerobatics at air shows every year. Aerobatics are amazing flying maneuvers such as rolls and loops.

The Thunderbirds team performs precision formation and solo flying routines in six F-16 Falcons. One part of their show is the four-aircraft diamond formation. The formation displays the precision of Air Force pilots. The

The USAF Thunderbirds Demonstration Team performs the four-aircraft diamond formation.

solo routines highlight the capabilities of the F-16 Fighting Falcon jet and its pilots.

The Thunderbirds also represent the United States and its armed forces to foreign nations and project international goodwill. They are called America's Ambassadors in Blue.

The F-22 Raptor

The single-seat F-22 Raptor is the newest stealth fighter jet in the Air Force. Many of the details of the F-22 Raptor remain classified top secret, but we do know some things about the Raptor. It is 62 feet long, and its two engines are the most powerful fighter engines in the world. It is the first fighter with thrust-vectoring exhaust nozzles for control. This means that the pilot can point the exhaust gases from the tailpipe either to the left or right, or up and down, instead of having the gases go straight out. This allows the pilot to change the direction of the airplane more quickly while traveling at supersonic speeds.[5] *Supersonic* means "faster than the speed of sound." The speed of sound is about 750 miles per hour at sea level and 650 miles per hour at high altitudes.

Most fighters can fly to about 50,000 feet. The Raptor can fly at up to 66,000 feet.[6] Because the F-22 is a stealth

Two F-22 Raptors are lining up to be refueled by a KC-135 Stratotanker. The F-22 is the latest stealth fighter in the Air Force.

fighter, it carries all its bombs and missiles inside the plane, not on its wings. It can drop its satellite-guided bombs and missiles to within 30 feet of a target. It is also a fly-by-wire airplane. *Fly-by-wire* means that there are special electronic circuits operated by a computer (instead of control cables) that move the flaps, elevators, and rudder.

The F-22 can fly faster than the speed of sound for as long as thirty minutes, longer than any other fighter. It can fly over enemy territory faster and longer. Since it is a stealth airplane, it cannot be detected by enemy radar.

CHAPTER 3

Bombers

In May 1998, twelve pilots sat in the briefing room at Whiteman Air Force Base near Kansas City, Missouri. They were listening to the briefing officer outline their mission to Kosovo in the former Yugoslavia. The war in Kosovo had been going on for almost three months. Some of the things covered in the briefing were the order for each plane's midair refueling, what the targets looked like, and which airplanes would bomb what targets.

After the briefing, the pilots climbed aboard six sleek black B-2 bombers waiting in the hangars. Bombers are large jet airplanes that carry bombs and missiles. They are used to destroy enemy targets on the ground. Each B-2 has a crew of two pilots: an aircraft commander in the left seat, and a mission commander in the right seat. One of the first things the pilots do when they get aboard is plug in the optical disk, similar to a compact disk, that contains the mission information. The information is like an aerial road map showing the route through the air to the target.

≡ The B-2 Spirit

The B-2 was the world's first stealth bomber. It is made mostly of a carbon graphite material, which is stronger than steel and lighter than aluminum. This material also absorbs most of the radar energy. Each one of these four-engine bombers costs about $2 billion.

The heart of the B-2 bomber is the 36 onboard computers. The Spirit has more computer power than the space shuttle.[1] The B-2 relies on the computers to sneak in through enemy radar defenses. Exactly how it does this is classified information. Classified information is information that is kept secret so that an enemy does not find out about it.

After all the preflight checks are completed, the hangar doors open and six B-2 bombers taxi out to the runway. They are cleared for takeoff and head east, in pairs, one a little behind the other. Most of this flight is flown under control of the onboard computers, so only one pilot needs to be at the controls.

The round-trip to Kosovo takes about thirty hours, and the crews eat and sleep on board. Refueling takes place in

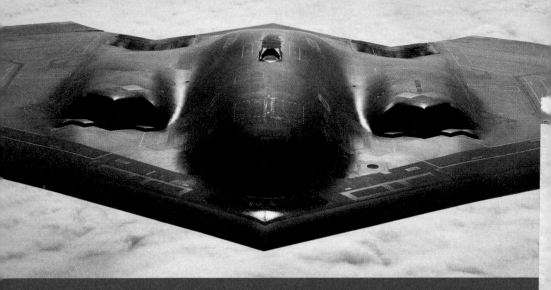

The B-2 bomber looks like no other airplane in the world. It is almost completely invisible to radar.

the air. The B-2 Spirit can fly at 650 miles per hour. To fly the 14,000-mile round-trip, the planes will refuel in the air four times.[2]

"For the two-man B-2 crews, the missions mean long hours and little sleep. Typically, each crew member gets between two and six hours of sleep during the thirty-hour flight," said General Leroy Barnidge, commander of the Air Force's only B-2 wing. "When they land, despite spending more than a day in the cramped . . . cockpit, they're excited and want to know when they can fly again."[3]

Built into the wall behind the left pilot seat is a device to make hot water for coffee or soup or to heat the hot-dog-and-chili combination the pilots call bomber dogs. There is a portable toilet under a seat cover, and a spot on the floor behind the two pilots' seats for one pilot to unroll a sleeping bag and lie down. "Simple things," said one pilot, "mean a lot when you are trying to stay alert on a long flight: some magazines, and catnaps." The pilots carry books, magazines, and coolers packed with water, juice, sandwiches, and cookies.

Each B-2 bomber can carry nuclear bombs or 40,000 pounds of regular bombs. But on this mission, they each carry a payload of 2,000-pound satellite-guided bombs. Once over a target, these "smart bombs" can hit within several yards of the target.

As the Spirit flight gets close to Europe, it will call the E-3 AWACS (Airborne Warning and Control System) Sentry flying somewhere over Europe. The E-3 will direct the B-2s over the target and watch for enemy fighters and missiles on their radar. (The AWACS are discussed in Chapter 5.)

Every time a B-2 flies a bombing mission, other aircraft support it. About fourteen hours into the mission, the B-2s meet up with other American warplanes. The Spirits fly to the targets with Navy EA-6B Prowlers, which will jam the enemy's radar. Because the Spirits do not carry missiles, the F-16 Falcons will protect the Spirits from enemy fighters.

After the B-2s drop their bombs, they head home. When they land, the pilots are debriefed. This means they are asked questions about what they saw and did. Then they take hot showers and go home to sleep.

In the eleven weeks of the air war, the six Spirits used over Kosovo flew a total of 45 missions and dropped more

The B-2 bomber has no tail and is basically a flying wing.

than 600 bombs. They were never seen by the enemy or hit by enemy fire.[4]

≡ *The B-1B Lancer*

The B-1B Lancer is another Air Force bomber. It has a crew of four: aircraft commander, pilot, offensive systems officer, and defensive systems officer. The bomber is 146 feet long and has four engines that enable it to fly faster than the speed of sound. The B-1B bomber holds the world record for the fastest round-the-world flight at 36 hours, 13 minutes.

The U.S. Air Force B-1B Lancer bomber leads a flight of Egyptian, French, Greek, Italian, and U.S. aircraft over the Great Pyramids of Giza, Egypt.

The Lancer can carry regular or nuclear bombs or ten cruise missiles. The cruise missiles use a computer program to fly at low altitudes and in and out of mountain passes to escape detection by enemy radar. A cruise missile can be launched from 530 miles away from the target. The B-1B Lancers flew 74 combat missions in Kosovo and dropped more than 5,000 bombs.

The B-52 Stratofortress

The B-52 is the workhorse of the bomber fleet. It has a crew of five: aircraft commander, pilot, a radar navigator, an electronic warfare officer, and a navigator. This eight-engine bomber has swept-back wings and can fly to 50,000 feet. It can travel 8,800 miles before it needs refueling. The wings are so long—the wingspan is 185 feet—that each wingtip has a landing wheel so that it does not scrape the ground. Its cruising speed is about 550 miles per hour.

The B-52 flew in the Vietnam War and Operation Desert Storm. During Operation Desert Storm, in 1991, it delivered 40 percent of all the bombs dropped.

CHAPTER 4

Tankers and Transports

Air Force tankers are like flying gas stations. They are used to refuel long-range bombers and fighters in the air. One of these tankers is the KC-10A Extender. It is similar to the DC-10 civilian airliner, but instead of having passenger seats, it is a giant flying fuel tank. The KC-10A Extender can carry 37,747 gallons of jet fuel. One KC-10A Extender can supply fuel for up to eight fighter airplanes. It carries a crew of four: a pilot, a copilot, a flight engineer, and a boom operator.

The flight engineer is responsible for the function of all the airplane's important systems. He watches all the gauges and dials on a panel in front of him, keeping track of

This is the view the boom operator has as the B-2 Spirit refuels. The small wings on the boom help guide it into the fuel opening on the B-2.

vital information such as engine oil pressure, fuel flow, engine temperatures, and engine speeds.

During aerial refueling, the boom operator, who is called Boomer, helps guide a large pipe called a boom down from the tanker. It will hook up with a receiving aircraft, such as a B-2 Spirit heading to Kosovo.

After the B-2 Spirit makes radio contact with a KC-10A, the B-2 bombers have to slow down so that they can hook up and refuel with the tanker. The sky is dark: the only lights are the dim navigation lights on each aircraft. The navigation lights are the red light on the left wing, the green light on the right wing, and the white flashing light on the tail. They are the same kind of lights that airliners have. The pilots must watch the navigation lights on the other aircraft so that they do not crash into each other.

Every move has been planned and practiced, but the pilots still have to be very careful during aerial refueling. They have to keep their airplanes steady in the turbulence while traveling at more than 300 miles per hour at 35,000 feet. This is dangerous work, and it takes skill and nerve.

Sitting in the rear of the tanker aircraft beneath the tail, the boom operator can see the B-2 receiver aircraft through a wide window. Boomer is in radio contact with each airplane taking on fuel. The hookup is made by directions given through a system of lights located on the wings and belly of the tanker. These lights tell the pilot of the bomber if he should go to the left or right to make the connection with the boom.

After each Spirit is refueled, it continues its flight to Kosovo, and the tanker heads back to base for another load of fuel.

Although the KC-10A's primary mission is aerial refueling, it is also used as a cargo plane. It can refuel fighters and, at the same time, carry the support personnel and equipment the fighters need. The KC-10A can transport up to 75 people and nearly 170,000 pounds of cargo a distance of about 4,400 miles.

≡ Transports

Transports are large airplanes that carry supplies, weapons, and soldiers to distant places around the world. The four-engine C-5 Galaxy transport is the largest transport airplane in the Air Force. It is the airplane that carries up to four presidential limousines when the President travels. It can carry 261,000 pounds of cargo— that is over 130 tons—for 3,500 miles, or fly indefinitely with aerial refueling.[2] The Galaxy is a "drive-through" airplane. Its nose lifts up and a door in the back folds down for both nose and tail loading. The C-5 is 243 feet long, and its 223-foot wingspan is just eight feet shorter than the entire length of Air Force One.

The Galaxy has a crew of seven: a pilot, a copilot, two flight engineers, and three loadmasters. The flight engineers' job is to watch the airplane's systems, by keeping track of vital information such as fuel flow. They make sure the fuel is transferred from the fuel tanks to the engines properly. If this were not done, the airplane could become unbalanced and dangerous to fly.

The loadmasters are responsible for the loading and unloading of the cargo. It is their job to make sure the airplane is loaded correctly, that the load is balanced, and that the airplane is not damaged during this process.

The C-5 has three major compartments. The forward upper deck seats a cockpit crew of four: a pilot, a copilot, and two flight engineers. Because it flies for long periods, it may also have a relief crew. It has two bunk rooms with three beds in each. There is another compartment called

The C-5 Galaxy is the largest cargo airplane in the Air Force. Here it is unloading a Black Hawk helicopter.

the courier compartment with eight seats. This forward upper deck, called the flight deck, also has a galley and a toilet.

Behind the wing on the upper deck is the second compartment. It has seats for 75 more people. It also has a galley and two toilets.

The third compartment is the cargo compartment. The floor is 121 feet long and can hold six transcontinental buses, two M1-A1 Abrams battle tanks, seven UH-1 Huey helicopters, or 270 passengers. It could also carry 348 grand pianos, or eight bowling alley lanes.

≡ The C-130 Hercules

The C-130 Hercules is a four-engine turboprop. A turboprop is a propeller-driven airplane that uses jet turbine engines. The Hercules has a crew of four: a pilot, a copilot, a flight engineer, and a navigator. Sometimes it also carries a loadmaster.

The Hercules flies at about 360 miles per hour. It can fly as high as 33,000 feet and carry about 38,000 pounds of cargo. Although its primary role is for troop and cargo

An air-to-air front view of a AC-130 Spectre gunship aircraft in flight.

The C-17 is the latest cargo airplane in the Air Force. Its four engines are so powerful that it can back up on the ground, and even go backward up a small incline.

transport, it also serves as a gunship, tanker, and rescue aircraft.

The C-17 Globemaster

The C-17 Globemaster is the newest Air Force cargo airplane. It is 174 feet long and has a 170-foot wingspan. It can carry 172,000 pounds of cargo at 41,000 feet and 575 miles per hour. It also flies troops. Its four engines are so powerful that it can back up on the ground, even up a small incline. There are three crew members on the Globemaster: a pilot, a copilot, and a loadmaster. It has bulletproof panels on the floor of the cockpit to protect the pilots from small arms fire when landing or taking off in enemy territory. It is also a fly-by-wire airplane.

CHAPTER 5

Special Airplanes

The Air Force uses airplanes with special electronics equipment such as radar, infrared sensors, and powerful cameras to control battle tactics and to look down on enemy territory.

The E-3 AWACS (Airborne Warning and Control System) Sentry is an airborne command and control center for the Air Force. It is like a flying radar station. Like a traffic cop who tells cars where to go, it tells fighters and bombers where to attack in enemy territory. It does this from hundreds of miles away using special electronics equipment such as infrared heat-seeking sensors and cameras that can photograph enemy positions through the clouds, in any weather conditions, and at night. The Sentry can see and track air and sea targets at the same time.

The Sentry controls fighter and bomber attacks from 35,000 feet high and as far away as 300 miles. It also guides fighters and bombers safely out of enemy territory after a mission. It keeps a lookout for enemy fighters or missiles and warns friendly planes if the enemy launches fighters or missiles.

The Sentry is a military version of the Boeing 707 passenger airliner. The major difference is the huge 30-foot-wide and 6-foot-thick rotating radar dome on top. This radar "eye" has a 360-degree view of the horizon and can "see" more than 300 miles in any direction.

There are two antennas inside the dome. One is for the radar system and the other for the identification-friend-or-foe (IFF) system. The IFF tells the operators if an aircraft they see on radar is a friendly aircraft or the enemy. Each airplane has a special code it automatically transmits to the AWACS. The AWACS knows which airplanes are the friendly ones by the codes it receives.

The beams from this radar allow controllers to see the ground surface, to identify ships and low-flying planes, and to detect missiles in the stratosphere. The stratosphere is a part of Earth's atmosphere. It begins at about 37,000 feet above the surface and continues to about 164,000 feet.

The Sentry carries a crew of four: a pilot, a copilot, a navigator, and a flight engineer. It also carries up to nineteen radar technicians per mission. The radar technicians perform the jobs of surveillance, identification, weapons control, battle management, and communications. They use computer consoles, which show radar data on video screens.

The technicians are divided into two sections, the surveillance section and the control section. They are like people in an airport control tower. In the surveillance section, technicians keep track of friendly planes, such as the B-2s, when they enter the area controlled by the Sentry. It is a radar technician's job to guide the bombers through the area where other warplanes are flying. The technicians monitor the airspace and pass on information to the weapons controllers in the control section.

In the control section, the weapons controllers sit at radarscopes. They guide friendly aircraft such as the F-16 toward enemy planes if they should appear.[1]

The Sentry directs the F-16 Falcons to fly top cover high above a B-2 Spirit flight. If the Sentry detects enemy aircraft, it will guide the F-16s to them so that the Falcons can destroy them with guided missiles.

The E-3 AWACS played a key role in the success of Operation Desert Storm. From January 16 until the February 27, 1991 cease-fire, four U.S. Air Force AWACS aircraft were continuously airborne, controlling more than 3,000 airplanes each day.

The SR-71 Blackbird

The Lockheed SR-71 is known as the Blackbird because it is painted black. It is 107 feet long, 18 feet high, and has a 55-foot wingspan. This was the first stealth-like aircraft in the Air Force. The Air Force uses it as a spy plane. It flies high over enemy territory, out of the range of most missiles, and photographs enemy targets. It is the fastest and highest-flying airplane in the world. Its engines, equivalent to 45 diesel locomotives, allow it to cruise for long periods above Mach 3.[2] That is more than 2,250 miles per hour, similar to flying at 37 miles per minute or 3,300 feet per second. It is capable of flying from Los Angeles to New York in about an hour.

The SR-71 Blackbird is the fastest airplane in the world. Although its maximum altitude and speed are classified, we know that it can fly to over 80,000 feet (15 miles) high.

The Blackbird flies so fast that the temperature on the outside of the fuselage reaches more than 1,200 degrees Fahrenheit. The aircraft is built totally of titanium alloy and incorporates original stealth technology. The paint is designed to absorb radar energy. The shape of the Blackbird is also designed to fool radar. Its tail, wings, and fuselage are built to trap radar energy.

The Blackbird has two jet engines and carries a crew of two: a pilot and a reconnaissance systems officer (RSO). The RSO monitors the aircraft systems and the special electronic spy equipment. The plane does not carry bombs or missiles because it is a spy plane and not a fighter or bomber.

Active USAF Aircraft

The numerous types of Air Force aircraft serve many roles today. This table lists all the aircraft currently flown by the Air Force. The aircraft fly fighter and bombing missions, transport troops and supplies, and refuel airplanes in the air. They also fly the President and keep an eye on the world with their spy planes.

Bombers

B-1B Lancer—A four-engine bomber that can fly at supersonic speeds and carry nuclear bombs. Holds the world record for the fastest round-the-world flight.

B-2 Spirit—The world's first stealth bomber. With 86 onboard computers, it has more computer power than the space shuttle.

B-52 Stratofortress—An eight-engine bomber that has swept-back wings and can travel 8,800 miles before it needs refueling. The wings are so long that each wingtip has a landing wheel so that it does not scrape the ground.

Cargo/Transport

C-141 Starlifter—The first pure jet designed for cargo. Its 93-foot-long cargo bay can hold up to 208 ground troops or 166 paratroops.

C-130 Hercules—A four-engine turboprop that flies at about 360 miles per hour and as high as 33,000 feet. It can carry about 38,000 pounds of cargo.

C-17 Globemaster III—The newest Air Force cargo airplane. It is 174 feet long and can carry 172,000 pounds of cargo at 41,000 feet and 575 miles per hour.

C-5A/B Galaxy—The largest transport airplane in the Air Force, used to carry up to four presidential limousines when the President travels.

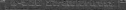
B-52G Stratofortress

C-141 Starlifter

Fighters

F-117A Nighthawk—The world's first stealth fighter, made with flat panels placed at angles to scatter the radar away from the airplane and out into space.

F-15 Eagle—A single-seat, twin-engine jet fighter that can fly up to 1,650 miles per hour. It can carry one 20-mm cannon with 940 rounds and eight Sidewinder air-to-air missiles.

F-16 Fighting Falcon—A 49-foot-long fighter that can fly to 50,000 feet at speeds up to 1,500 miles per hour. One pilot sits in a bubble canopy for greater visibility.

F-111 Aardvark—A fighter-bomber capable of supersonic speeds. It can operate as low as treetop level or as high as 60,000 feet.

F-22 Raptor—The newest stealth fighter in the Air Force. It can fly at supersonic speeds for as long as thirty minutes, longer than any other fighter.

A-10 Thunderbolt—Nicknamed the Warthog, it is the first Air Force aircraft specially designed for close air support of ground forces. It has heavy armor and a high-velocity 30-mm cannon.

Helicopters

HH-3E Jolly Green Giant—A twin-engine, heavy-lift helicopter used for search-and-recovery of personnel, combat, and special operations.

MH-53J Pave Low III—The largest and most powerful helicopter in the Air Force. It has special radar that enables the crew to follow terrain contours and avoid obstacles.

MH-60G Pave Hawk—Used to resupply Special Operations forces in day, night, or bad weather conditions. Other missions include combat search and rescue.

F-15 Eagle

MH-53 Pave Low

UH-1N Huey—A twin-engine helicopter that is used for airlift of emergency security and disaster response forces, space shuttle landing support, search-and-rescue operations, and public affairs flights.

UH-1H Iroquois—A light-lift helicopter used as a distinguished visitor transport.

Tankers

KC-10A Extender—Carries 37,747 gallons of jet fuel and can hold passengers and cargo.

KC-130 Hercules—A tanker/transport that provides in-flight refueling to tactical aircraft and helicopters, as well as rapid ground refueling when required.

KC-135 Stratotanker—Like the Boeing 707 airliner, but it carries 31,275 gallons of jet fuel instead of passengers.

Trainers

T-1A Jayhawk—A medium-range, twin-engine jet used to train student pilots to fly transport or tanker aircraft.

T-37 Tweet—A twin-engine jet used for training student pilots and navigators in instrumentation, formation, and night flying.

T-38 Talon—An advanced twin-engine, high-altitude, supersonic jet used in a variety of training roles.

T-43A—A Boeing 737 jet. It is a medium-range, swept-wing jet aircraft used to train navigators.

KC-130J Hercules

T-37 Tweet

Special-Use Aircraft

Air Force One—A Boeing 747 that provides air transportation for the President of the United States. Also, any other plane that is carrying the President.

AC-130U Spectre—A Hercules gunship armed with 25-mm and 40-mm cannons and a 105-mm gun. It is used against enemy troops on the ground.

C-9A/C Nightingale—A twin-engine, medium-range, swept-wing jet aircraft used mostly for medical evacuation missions.

C-20A/B Gulfstream III—A twin-engine jet that flies high-ranking government and Defense Department officials.

C-32A—A Boeing 757 that can carry the Vice President, cabinet members of the executive branch of the government, high-ranking military personnel, and members of Congress when traveling on government business.

E-3 AWACS Sentry—An airborne command and control center. It guides fighters and bombers attacking in enemy territory.

MC-130P Combat Shadow—Flies secret low-level missions into enemy territory to provide air refueling for Special Operations helicopters. It also air-drops small Special Operations teams into areas behind enemy lines.

SR-71 Blackbird—The fastest and highest-flying spy plane in the world. It can fly at speeds of more than 2,250 miles per hour and higher than 80,000 feet.

U-2R/U-2S Angel—A single-seat, single-engine, high-altitude spy plane. Because it flies at high altitude, the pilot must wear a full pressure suit.

V-22 Tiltrotor—An aircraft that takes off and lands like a helicopter. Once airborne, its engines can be rotated to convert the aircraft to a turboprop capable of high-speed, high-altitude flight.

AC-130U Spectre

U-2R/U-2S Angel

Chapter Notes

Chapter 1. Air Force One

1. *Air Force One—A History* (New York: A&E Television Networks, 1997).

2. Walter Sorrells, "The President's New Plane," *Popular Mechanics*, October 1991, p. 47.

3. *Air Force One: Flight II—The Planes and the Presidents*, Sluham Productions (Orlando Park, Ill.: MPI Home Video 1991.

4. Ibid.

5. Daniel P. George, "The Flying White House," *Boys' Life*, February 1995, p. 14.

6. George Bush, "Man Oh Man Was It Comfortable," *Forbes*, Winter 1996, p. 120.

Chapter 2. Fighters

1. Paul F. Crickmore and Alison J. Crickmore, *F-117 Nighthawk* (Osceola, Wis.: Motorbooks International Publishing Co., 1999), pp. 108–109.

2. *Stealth Technology* (New York: The History Channel A&E Television Networks, 1997).

3. James C. Goodall, *America's Stealth Fighters and Bombers: B-2, F-117, YF-22 and YF-23* (Osceola, Wis.: Motorbooks International Publishing Co., 1992), p. 15.

4. Crickmore, pp. 109, 167.

5. Bill Sweetman, *F-22 Raptor* (Osceola, Wis.: Motorbooks International Publishing Co., 1998), p. 51.

6. Ibid., p. 45.

Chapter 3. Bombers

1. *Stealth Technology* (New York: The History Channel A&E Television Networks, 1997).

2. William Matthews, "B-2s Running a Commuter War," *Air Force Times*, May 17, 1999, p. 18.

3. Ibid.

4. Robert Wall, "Pentagon Details Flaws in Kosovo Weapons," *Aviation Week & Space Technology*, February 21, 2000, p. 43.

Chapter 4. Tankers and Transports

1. Nicholas A. Veronico and Jim Dunn, *Giant Cargo Planes* (Osceola, Wis.: Motorbooks International Publishing Co., 1999), p. 51.

2. Ibid.

Chapter 5. Special Airplanes

1. G. W. Poindexter, "Life Aboard an AWACS," *Air Force Times*, July 25, 1994, p. 12.

2. Paul F. Crickmore, *Lockheed SR-71: The Secret Missions Exposed*, Rev. ed. (London: Osprey Aerospace, 1997), p. 45.

aerobatics—Flying maneuvers, such as loops and rolls, performed with an aircraft.

AWACS—Airborne Warning and Control System; a flying radar station. It tells fighters and bombers where to attack in enemy territory.

control surfaces—The movable parts of the tail and wings, such as the rudder, flaps, and elevators; these enable the aircraft to fly and maneuver.

flight engineer—The person responsible for monitoring the airplane's systems by keeping track of vital information such as the fuel flow.

fly-by-wire—The use of electronic circuits to operate the plane's control surfaces.

galley—A small kitchen.

loadmaster—The person responsible for the loading and unloading of the cargo from an aircraft.

Mach number—The ratio of the speed of an object through air to the speed of sound. Mach 1 is equal to the speed of sound, about 750 miles per hour at sea level and 650 miles per hour at high altitudes. Mach 2 is two times the speed of sound.

payload—The items carried by an aircraft, such as passengers or instruments necessary to the flight.

radar—Radio detecting and ranging. A device that emits radio waves and processes their reflections on a monitor. The information tells the operator an object's location and velocity.

reconnaissance—An inspection of enemy territory.

SAM—Surface-to-air missile; a ground-launched heat-seeking missile.

stealth—Technology that incorporates different ways of hiding objects from detection.

stratosphere—The part of Earth's atmosphere that begins at about 37,000 feet above the surface and continues to 164,000 feet.

supersonic—Faster than the speed of sound.

tankers—Large airplanes that carry thousands of gallons of jet fuel.

transports—Large cargo airplanes that carry supplies and weapons.

turboprop—A propeller-driven airplane that uses a jet turbine engine.

wingman—The pilot who flies behind the right wing of his flight leader.

Further Reading

Books

Chant, Christopher. *Military Aircraft*. Broomall, Pa.: Chelsea House Publishers, 1999.

Hansen, Ole S. *Aircraft*. Orlando, Fl.: Raintree Steck-Vaughn Publishers, 1998.

Jarrett, Philip. *Ultimate Aircraft*. New York: Dorling Kindersley Publishing, Inc., 2000.

Maynard, Christopher. *Aircraft*. Minneapolis: The Lerner Publishing Group, 1999.

Schleifer, Jay. *Fighter Planes*. Mankato, Minn.: Capstone Press, Inc., 1996.

Sullivan, George A. *Modern Fighter Planes*. New York: Facts on File, 1991.

Internet Addresses

Andrews Air Force Base. *Air Force One*. June 1996. <http://www.andrews.af.mil/Vc25a.htm> (January 23, 2001).

Edwards Air Force Base. April 5, 2000. <http://www.edwards.af.mil/gallery/index.html> (January 23, 2001).

International Women's Air and Space Museum. © 1996–2000. <http://www.iwasm.org/> (January 23, 2001).

Lundgren, Johan. *Airliners.net*. © 1996–2000. <http://www.airliners.net> (January 23, 2001).

National Aeronautics and Space Administration. *Off to a Flying Start*. "Introduction to Flight." December 27, 1999. <http://ltp.larc.nasa.gov/flyingstart/module1.html> (January 23, 2001).

Smithsonian National Air and Space Museum. © 2000. <http://www.nasm.edu> (January 23, 2001).

U.S. Air Force. *Air Force Link*. n.d. <http://www.af.mil> (January 23, 2001).

Index